Contents

1 | Life in Britain in 1906

In 1906 the majority of people believed that Great Britain was the most powerful country in the world. Although Britain was a small island, it ruled an **empire** which stretched around the globe. Britain ruled one quarter of all the people in the world. It was still one of the leading industrial countries in the world. Indeed most people in Britain still considered it to be the world's leading country. However both Germany and the USA had overtaken Britain's industrial production by 1906.

A The British Empire.

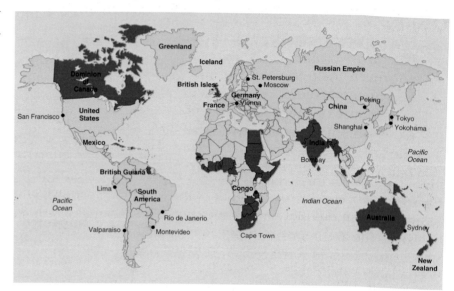

The period covered by this book is only 12 years but there was a great deal of change during this time. Firstly, in 1906 a new government took power which was committed to improving the standard of living of the poorest section of the population. Secondly, the First World War had a massive impact on British society. For the first time the entire resources of Britain and almost its entire population were actively involved in contributing towards eventual victory.

In the early nineteenth century Britain had been a mainly rural country with a population of about 10 million. Most people had lived in villages and many of them had worked on the land. By 1906 this had all changed. The population had increased to about 42 million and only about 9 per cent of workers had jobs in agriculture. Most people now lived in towns. In 1801 there had only been 16 towns with a population of more than 20 000. By 1906 there were almost 160.

Transport was changing as well. There were very few cars in Britain and the horse was still the main form of transport. Until 1896 any car had to be accompanied by a man walking in front carrying a red flag. There was little point in owning a car if it could only go as fast as a man could walk. However, the horse did face competition in public transport. By 1906 most towns and cities had introduced electric powered trams.

Rich and poor

In 1906 there were almost no houses with electricity. This meant that there were none of the domestic appliances that we take for granted today. However, this did not matter if you were rich. You were able to employ servants to do all the domestic work.

About 3 per cent of the population could be described as being very rich. These were the people who earned at least £700 a year. They included the great landowners, wealthy industrialists and the most successful professional men, such as senior judges and senior officers in the armed forces.

Below the rich came the middle classes. They might earn between £150 and £700 a year. This would still mean that most of them could employ at least one servant. These people were the shop-keepers and professional people such as lawyers.

The working class made up the rest of the population. The average wage for men who worked in industry was only £1.50 a week and women earned much less. Most of this would go on rent and food. In a survey of York the businessman Rowntree reckoned that a family with three children needed just over £1 a week to cope. He discovered that 40 per cent of the working class in York earned less than this. But even an income of £1 left families with no money for medical expenses, or for any luxuries such as alcohol or gambling. Since people did fall ill, drink and gamble, many more than 40 per cent of families were living in poverty.

Britain in 1906 was a land of contrasts. Life might have been extremely comfortable for the rich, but it was very tough for the majority of the population.

B A rich English family relaxing.

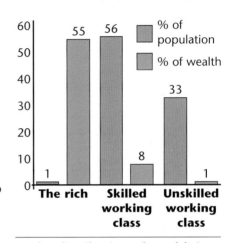

D The distribution of wealth in 1906, according to the Liberal MP Chiozza Money.

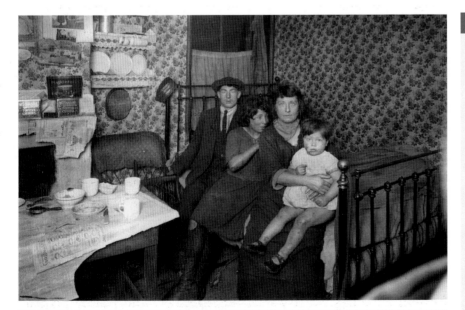

C A working-class family living in a one-room tenement in Bethnal Green, London. Many poor people lived in such cramped conditions.

QUESTIONS

1 Look at source A. Why do you think the British felt that Britain was the most powerful country in the world?

2 Study sources B and C. What differences can you see in the lives of the people shown in each photograph?

3 How might someone use sources B, C and D to support the view that Britain in 1906 was a very divided and unjust society? You may also include material from the text to back up your answer.

2 | How was Britain Governed in 1906?

1832	7%
1867	16%
1884	29%

A The percentage of adults who could vote.

1906	Conservative
	Liberal
1915	
1918	Coalition of Conservatives and Labour with Liberal Lloyd George as Prime Minister.

B The governments of 1900–18.

Parliament

Britain in 1906 was a parliamentary democracy, just like it is today. This means that a parliament, elected by the people, makes all the laws. Even the King, Edward VII, could not reject a decision made by parliament. However, in many respects things were very different. Governments at this time tended to contain a large number of lords. Indeed the unelected House of Lords was able to block decisions made by the elected House of Commons. Today the House of Lords can only delay measures and the Prime Minister cannot be a member of the Lords.

Who could vote?

Today everyone over the age of 18 can vote. This was not the situation in 1906, although things had changed dramatically in the previous 100 years. In 1806 very few people could vote and the system was very unfair. It did not reflect the change in the country which the **Industrial Revolution** had produced. However, the parliamentary Acts of 1832, 1867 and 1884 did greatly increase the number of men who could vote. By 1906 all male householders could vote. This meant that over 5 million men could vote, just under one third of the adult population. However, no women could vote in parliamentary elections until 1918. The story of their campaign is told in Chapter 6. Though many people could now vote most MPs came from wealthy backgrounds. They needed to be rich since an MP was not paid.

The political parties

The two main parties in Britain in 1906 were the Liberals and the Conservatives. They had dominated politics for much of the nineteenth century and expected to dominate in the twentieth century as well. They represented the interests of different types of rich people. The Liberals tended to be supported by wealthy businesspeople and the Conservatives by landowners and other businesspeople.

The Conservative Party believed that the government should let the rich get on with the job of making Britain richer. The government should not interfere with the economy. This was known as *laissez faire*. It meant **free trade**, that is, no duties on imported or exported goods.

However, British industries were finding it increasingly difficult to compete with Germany and America and so some people wanted to introduce import duties to make foreign goods more expensive in Britain. This would protect British industries from foreign competition at home, yet it would hurt Britain's exports, as other

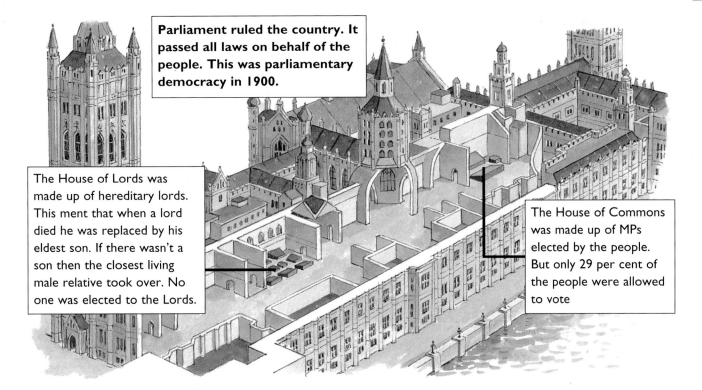

Parliament ruled the country. It passed all laws on behalf of the people. This was parliamentary democracy in 1900.

The House of Lords was made up of hereditary lords. This ment that when a lord died he was replaced by his eldest son. If there wasn't a son then the closest living male relative took over. No one was elected to the Lords.

The House of Commons was made up of MPs elected by the people. But only 29 per cent of the people were allowed to vote

C Parliament in the early twentieth century.

countries would retaliate by putting up their duties on British goods. One group of Conservative MPs, led by Joseph Chamberlain, wanted to increase import duties on German and American goods in order to protect trade within the empire. But the issue divided the party and led to the Conservatives being defeated in the 1906 election.

The Liberals believed in the freedom of the individual. They believed that wealth was created through the hard work of individuals. Therefore the government should play only a small role and should not get in the way of the businesspeople who created wealth. Many Liberals were Christians but not members of the Church of England. Many of them believed in temperance, that is not drinking alcohol, because it stopped people working hard and doing their duty.

The Liberal and Conservative parties both represented the interests of the rich and the middle classes. There was no party to represent the working class. This was hardly surprising. For most of the nineteenth century the working class did not have the right to vote. A number of **socialist** societies were formed and in 1900 they joined with some trade unions to form the Labour Representative Committee (LRC). However in the October 1900 General Election only two LRC candidates were elected to parliament. In 1906 the LRC changed its name to the Labour Party. However, in many areas of the country people didn't have the chance to vote Labour because the party lacked money and so couldn't afford to support many candidates.

QUESTIONS

1 Read the text in this chapter. In what ways has the House of Lords lost power since the early 1900s?

2 Why did British workers feel it was necessary to create the Labour Party?

3 Study source C. What is a parliamentary democracy? Use the text as well as the source to explain your answer.

4 How democratic was Britain in 1906? Use sources A and B as well as the text to explain your answer. Think about:

• who could vote and who could not
• the House of Lords

3 | The Reforms of the Liberal Government

Key Issue

Why did the Liberal government introduce reforms to help the young, old and unemployed?

Along with the Conservatives, the other major political party was the Liberal Party. The Liberals won a huge victory in the 1906 election. They won 401 seats compared with the Conservatives who won just 157. The Labour Party won 29 seats. This was an amazing victory after two decades of Conservative governments. The 'New Liberal' Party of 1906 promised to introduce social reforms to help the old and the weak. It was a message the voters wanted to hear and Henry Campbell-Bannerman became the new Prime Minister. But why was the Liberal Party suddenly promising to improve people's standard of living? The party had been in government before but had not made these changes.

A The Worker's Emancipation. A New Liberal Election postcard from 1910. Emancipation means freedom.

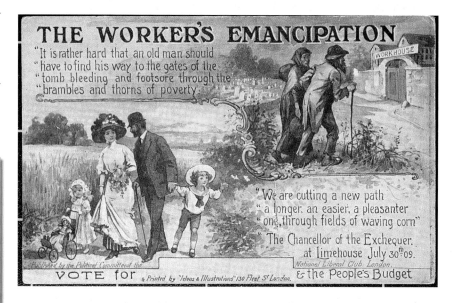

B Lloyd George, the Liberal Chancellor of the Exchequer, speaking in 1909.

Help for the aged and the deserving poor – it is time it was done. It is a shame that a rich country like ours – probably the richest in the world – should allow those who have toiled [worked hard] all their days to end in poverty and starvation.

New Liberalism

The creators of this 'New Liberalism' were David Lloyd George and Winston Churchill. They had a number of reasons for wanting to turn the Liberal Party into the party of reform.

- One reason was that some people in the Liberal Party realised that the rise of the Labour Party was a sign that working people were not happy with the two big parties. Both hoped that concern for the poor would win votes from people who were turning to the Labour Party.

- Lloyd George was born in a Welsh village and hated the English upper classes. He really wanted to improve the conditions of ordinary people. In an age when MPs were not paid, most MPs were already rich men before becoming MPs. Lloyd George was unusual in not being rich.

- The work of social investigators such as Charles Booth and Seebohm Rowntree had revealed the true extent of poverty in England (see pages 8–9). They had shown disease, unemployment and old age to be the causes of poverty, and not laziness as many people previously believed.

C Winston Churchill, writing in 1901.

I have been reading a book by Mr Rowntree called *Poverty* which has impressed me very much ... it is evident from the figures that the American labourer is a stronger, larger, healthier, better fed and consequently more efficient animal than a large proportion of our own population ... I see little glory in an empire which rules the waves, and is unable to flush its sewers.

■ Lloyd George had visited Germany, the country which was quickly developing into the new industrial leader of Europe. Germany already had health insurance and old age pensions. It was hoped that the reforms in Britain would produce a stronger and fitter workforce, which would be able to meet the challenge of Germany. Unless the living conditions of working people were improved then Germany would become a more important industrial power and Britain would no longer lead the world.

■ Between 1899 and 1902 Britain was at war in South Africa. Half the men who volunteered to go and fight were simply not fit enough to fight. If Britain was to remain the most powerful country in the world it needed an army capable of defending its empire. That meant much healthier people.

What were the problems facing the Liberals?

Education

Education was vital if Britain was to have a modern workforce. By 1900 every child did go to school. In 1899 the school leaving age was raised to 12 and this meant that every child received a basic education at an elementary school. However, only about one child in 80 went on to secondary school. Secondary education was not free and so most working-class people couldn't afford it. Of course the very rich sent their sons to public schools, which aimed to turn out perfect Christian English gentlemen, and most middle-class families did send their children to secondary school. But, in Germany, far more children attended secondary school. As far as education was concerned, Britain was losing out to its new rival. As industries became more complex an educated workforce was needed. However, some people thought it was wrong to educate working-class children. They believed that educated working-class children would not want to work in factories. Educated workers would become dissatisfied with their life and then they would rebel. In 1902 the Conservative Education Act brought education under the control of local councils and gave them the power to open secondary schools as well, but they were still not free.

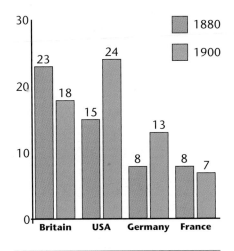

D The percentage share of the world manufacturing output – this means goods made by machines.

E The report of the Royal Commission on Technical Instruction in 1884. This was an investigation set up by the government.

The one point in which Germany is overwhelmingly superior to England is in schools . . .

The dense ignorance so common among workmen in England is unknown.

QUESTIONS

1 Study source A. What reasons does it give to suggest that people should vote for the Liberals?

2 Study sources B and C. Do they support the reasons given in source A?

3 Do you believe that source A is a reliable picture of Britain in 1910?

4 In what way does source C support the point made in source D?

5 'The main reason that the Liberals wanted to introduce reforms was to win the next election.' Using the sources and the text explain whether or not you agree with this statement.

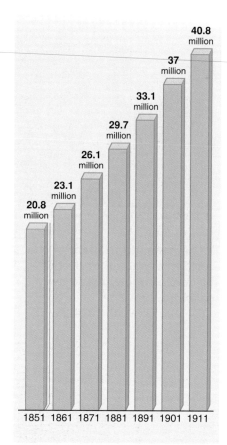

40.8 million
37 million
33.1 million
29.7 million
26.1 million
23.1 million
20.8 million

1851 1861 1871 1881 1891 1901 1911

F The rise in the British population.

Poverty

At the beginning of the twentieth century many British people lived in terrible conditions. Part of the reason for this can be seen in source F. The population of Britain had risen dramatically in the second half of the nineteenth century. However, it was not simply the number of people which created the problem. It was where they were living. There were fewer and fewer jobs in the countryside. Therefore people were forced to live in towns in the hope of finding jobs.

By 1906 towns were very overcrowded. While in 1801 only 25 per cent of the population lived in towns of more than 10 000 people, by 1906, 75 per cent of the British people lived in such towns. The result was terrible conditions. Many people were forced to live in slum housing. Overcrowding and poor sanitation, for example a lack of toilets, produced disease. By 1913 half a million people a year were still dying from diseases such as pneumonia, bronchitis and tuberculosis.

At the opening of the twentieth century Britain was arguably the richest country in the world. Yet for many of the working class the problem was not just that they lived in terrible conditions. They were often laid off when there was no work and this meant no money coming into the household. Once they were too old to work, there were no pensions for them. They were forced to rely on their family to help them survive. The governments of the nineteenth century had done very little to help people in such circumstances. They did not believe that it was the job of the government to get involved in ordinary people's lives.

Nevertheless, in 1875 the Public Health Act was introduced. This made it the duty of local councils to keep sewers clean and to remove rubbish from the streets. This was done in order to try and reduce the spread of disease. In the same year the government also gave councils the power to clear slums and replace them with better houses. However, although councils now had the power, they were not ordered to carry out slum clearance. Most councils did nothing.

I The rise in population in British towns and cities. Figures in thousands.

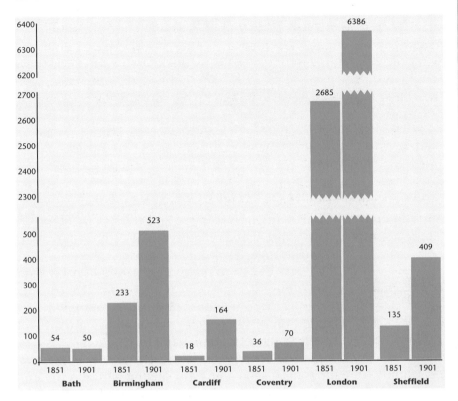

H Charles Booth describes the area around Covent Garden in London at the turn of the century.

Few of the 200 families who lived there occupied more than one room... Fifteen rooms out of twenty were filthy to the last degree. Not a room would be free from vermin. The little yard at the back was only sufficient for a dust-bin and closet and water-tap, serving six or seven families. The water would be drawn from cisterns which were receptacles for refuse, and perhaps the occasional dead cat.

J A Manchester slum at the end of the nineteenth century.

K A description of a house in York. Rowntree hired investigators to survey almost 50 000 people in York, about 66 per cent of the population. This was published in 1901.

Wooden floor of upper room has holes admitting numbers of mice. Roof very defective, the rain falling through on to the bed in wet weather. Outside wall also very damp. Plaster falling off. Tenants apparently clean.

Courtyard. Houses all back to back. Water supply for 12 houses from one tap placed in wall of privy (toilet).

QUESTIONS

1 Study sources F and G. Which do you feel is the more useful to a historian studying conditions in British cities?

2 Study sources I and H. Do they agree about conditions in British cities?

3 Study sources I and H. Is one source more reliable than the other about conditions in British cities?

4 Study sources J and K. Which source is the more useful in helping a historian to understand the conditions in British cities?

5 Study all the sources.

   'The years between 1900 and 1914 were years of great change and progress in Britain.' Do the sources and text support this interpretation?

Between 1906 and 1914 the Liberals introduced reforms in four main groups of people: the young, the old, the unemployed, and workers on low wages.

The Children's Charter

The Children's Charter is a name given to the 1908 Children and Young Persons Act. This meant that parents could be prosecuted for neglect. Special children's prisons, or borstals, were set up, so that children were no longer sent to adult prisons. This was after they were tried in special juvenile, rather than adult, courts. In addition, harsh penalties were set for anyone selling cigarettes or alcohol to children.

The government also passed series of acts between 1906 and 1908 dealing with the welfare of children. In 1906 an Act was passed which meant that local councils could provide school meals for poor children. However, it had limited effect because by 1914 fewer than half the education authorities in England and Wales were providing free meals. In 1914 the government made it compulsory to provide these meals and provided some money towards the cost. In 1907 another Act introduced medical inspections for all school children, so that those with illnesses could be identified. Local authorities were also allowed to provide free medical treatment for these children but most failed to do so. So, in 1912 the government provided the money so that ill children could receive treatment.

The 1907 Education Act also introduced scholarships for children from poor families. All secondary schools that received money from local government had to reserve 25 per cent of their places for pupils from elementary schools. The children were chosen by taking an examination.

The most important point about the Charter was that the government now recognised that children were entitled to good health and education as a right and not as charity.

The old

Before the introduction of old-age pensions, old people had to rely on their own savings and the generosity of their family in order to survive. Those who couldn't do this had to depend on charity.

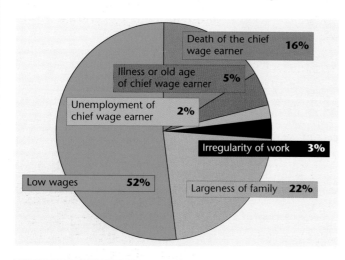

A Rowntree's findings on the causes of poverty in York in 1900. Rowntree hired investigators to survey almost 50 000 people in York, about 66 per cent of the population. They found that there were six main causes of poverty in York.

Death of the chief wage earner **16%**
Illness or old age of chief wage earner **5%**
Unemployment of chief wage earner **2%**
Irregularity of work **3%**
Low wages **52%**
Largeness of family **22%**

B Lloyd George, commenting on the National Insurance Act in a speech in June 1911.
I never said the Bill was a final solution. I am not putting it forward as a complete remedy. It is one of a series. We are advancing on the road, but it is an essential part of the journey.

The problem of the elderly was tackled when Lloyd George, the Chancellor of the Exchequer, introduced old-age pensions in 1908. The first pensions were paid on 1 January 1909. The Act gave a pension of 5 shillings (25 pence) a week to single people over 70 and 7 shillings 6d (37½ pence) to married couples. In the first year 650 000 people collected a pension from their post office. The full amount was only paid to those old people who earned less than £21 a year. Those earning between £21 and £31 were paid less on a gradually sliding scale.

The Labour Party complained that 5 shillings wasn't enough and that many people wouldn't live until 70 to draw their pensions. Despite this, the Act was still very popular with pensioners.

The unemployed and the low paid

Winston Churchill, President of the Board of Trade, introduced the first Labour Exchanges in 1909. Their purpose was to help unemployed people to find jobs. Before this the government gave no help to the unemployed looking for work. By 1913 there were already 430 exchanges in Britain but it was not compulsory for employers to tell exchanges that they had vacancies.

In 1906 the Liberal government introduced the Workmen's Compensation Act. This covered all workers who earned less than £250 a year. If they were badly injured by an accident at work they would still get half of their wages.

Much more significant was the National Insurance Act. Although medicine improved considerably in the nineteenth century it was not free. **Friendly societies** had been set up to provide health insurance but the poor and the unemployed could not afford to pay the premiums. In 1911 the National Insurance Act was introduced.

It allowed workers who earned less than £160 a year to see a doctor for free and to receive ten shillings a week if they were too sick to work. This was paid for by a fund into which workers, employers and the government all made payments.

In 1909 the Trade Boards Act was introduced by Churchill. It set a minimum wage for sweated industries, such as clothes-making , which were traditionally very low paid and had long hours. This affected only a small minority of workers – 400 000 by 1913.

How effective were the Liberal reforms?

The Liberal reforms established the foundations of the welfare state. After the Second World War, the Labour government would build on these foundations. But for now the reforms were just a beginning.

Firstly, medical care was only provided for the worker. It did not cover wives and children. Hospital treatment was not included and neither were dental and eye care. Secondly, the old-age pensions only covered people of 70 and over. This meant that there were still a lot of old people who got nothing at all. Finally, the unemployment insurance only covered about 2 million workers.

THE DAWN OF HOPE.

Mr. LLOYD GEORGE'S National Health Insurance Bill provides for the insurance of the Worker in case of Sickness.

Support the Liberal Government
in their policy of
SOCIAL REFORM.

C The Dawn of Hope. A Liberal Party election poster from 1911.

QUESTIONS

1 How far do sources B and C disagree about the effects of the Liberal reforms?

2 Source A gives six reasons for the causes of poverty in York. For each of the six causes, explain how the Liberal reforms may have helped to cure this problem. Use both the sources and the text to support your answer.

3 Study all the sources.

'By 1914 Britain had made no real progress in the fight against poverty.' Use the sources and the text to explain whether you agree or disagree with this view.

What was the Cost of Reform?

A **Rich Fare**, a *Punch* cartoon from 1909. Lloyd George is shown as a giant. The rich man (a plutocrat) is shown hiding under the table.

The Liberal reforms might not have helped everyone who needed help, but they were still going to cost a lot of money. At the same time Britain was engaged in an arms race with Germany. New battleships, known as Dreadnoughts, needed to be built. The reforms and the ships would together cost £15 million. Taxes would have to be increased. In 1909 the new Chancellor of the Exchequer, Lloyd George, presented what he called his 'People's Budget'. Income tax for rich people who earned more than £3000 a year would be increased from 1 shilling (5p) in every pound to 1 shilling 2d (6p). Those who earned less would only pay 9d (4p) in the pound.

Those who earned over £5000 a year would pay an extra super tax of a further 6d in the pound. On top of this death duties would be increased, along with land taxes. There was also to be a tax of 3d (just over 1p) in the pound on petrol and the car licence was introduced. Taxes on whisky and tobacco were also increased. The rich would most definitely have to pay for the reforms which would help the poorest people in the country.

To give an idea of how rich the people were paying the extra tax, the average wage for men at this time was just £94 a year. The Conservatives attacked the budget by calling it 'socialist'. The Labour Party criticised the budget for not going far enough. It wanted to redistribute wealth. That is it wanted to tax the rich and then make sure the money from those taxes was used to help all poor people and give them a reasonable standard of living.

B **Crescendo**. A *Punch* cartoon from May 1914.

C The fraud exposed. An election cartoon supporting the Conservatives, produced by the Budget Protest League. John Bull, on the left, representing the British people, is talking to Lloyd George on the right.

The House of Commons passed the budget but the mainly Conservative House of Lords rejected it. Without the support of the House of Lords these changes would not be legal. Lloyd George described the Lords as 'Mr Balfour's poodle' (Balfour was the leader of the Conservatives). The Prime Minister, Asquith, called two General Elections in 1910. The first to get the people's backing for the budget, the second to get the people's backing to reform the House of Lords. The Liberals won both elections but with much smaller majorities than in 1906.

The government then introduced the Parliament Act. The House of Lords was forced to agree that never again would it be able to defeat a budget. The Lords also had to agree that it could only delay, and not stop any other Bill passed by the House of Commons.

D *The Times* newspaper was read mostly by Conservatives. Here it is commenting on what it felt were the dangers of the introduction of free school meals for school children.

It will be said that we pay vast sums for teaching and feeding, but that the money is wasted if the children are not properly clad [clothed]. From that it is an easy step to paying for their proper housing.
The Times, 2 January 1905

E Lloyd George speaking about the House of Lords in 1909.

The question will be asked whether . . . [the House of Lords] . . . should override the judgement, the deliberate judgement, of millions of people who are engaged in the industry which makes the wealth of the country.

QUESTIONS

1 Look at the text. Why do you think Lloyd George described the House of Lords as 'Balfour's poodle'?

2 Why is the plutocrat (rich man) shown hiding under the table in source A?

3 Study sources A and B. Do they give the same impression of Lloyd George and his policies?

4 Why would Conservatives support the point being made by source C?

5 How reliable are sources C and D as evidence of attitudes to Lloyd George?

6 Study all the sources.

'The British people were strongly opposed to Lloyd George's 1909 "People's Budget". Do the sources support this interpretation? Use the sources and the text to explain your answer.

Votes for women

1?

Arguments for female suffrage

At the beginning of the twentieth century no woman could vote in elections for parliament. In 1911 only 60 per cent of adult males could vote. But many women were now demanding the right to vote. Source A shows some of the reasons why. Many women had wealth and careers and yet as long as they could not vote they felt that they were treated as second-class citizens. In 1867 parliament had discussed giving the vote to women, but on this and subsequent occasions, the male MPs had decided not to treat men and women equally.

Married Women's Property Act 1882. This gave women the right to own property separately from their husbands.

Since 1870 both boys and girls could attend primary schools. Also London and Cambridge Universities both gave places to women.

Women had been given the right to vote in local elections.

Women were increasingly getting jobs in banking and the civil service.

A Why were women demanding the right to vote?

B Suffragettes campaigning for votes for women.

Suffragists and Suffragettes

Although many women wanted the right to vote, they did not all agree on the best way to achieve their aim. In the nineteenth century the National Union of Women's Suffrage Societies (NUWSS) had been set up to demand the vote for women. It was mainly supported by wealthy women or those who had good jobs. The NUWSS was led by Millicent Fawcett and by 1914 had become a large organisation of 53 000 members.

The NUWSS's main concern was to get the vote for women on the same terms as men. In other words it was not campaigning for all adults to have the vote, only those who occupied houses. The members of the NUWSS were commonly known as Suffragists. They had both men and women as members, since some men felt that both men and women ought to have the right to vote. The NUWSS did not campaign for married women to be given the vote. Mrs Fawcett took the view that since married women by law had to obey their husbands, there was therefore no point in giving them the vote until the legal position of obedience had been changed.

In 1903 Emmeline Pankhurst, the daughter of a wealthy cotton manufacturer, set up the Women's Social and Political Union (WSPU). The members were more usually known as Suffragettes. Their slogan was 'Deeds not Words'. Only women were allowed to be members of the WSPU. The WSPU engaged in direct action. The purpose was to gain people's attention.

The Suffragettes became notorious for the actions they took to get their cause noticed. WSPU members took part in activities which scandalised many people, since women were not meant to behave in such ways. In 1905 Christabel Pankhurst, Emmeline's daughter, and Annie Kenney shouted out 'Votes for Women' during a speech by a government minister at the Manchester Free Trade Hall and they were arrested and imprisoned. This may not seem very outrageous today, but in 1905 it was considered very bad behaviour. In 1908 two Suffragettes chained themselves to the railing outside the Prime Minister's home at 10 Downing Street in London.

The government had suggested that it might introduce votes for women, so the WSPU called off its actions in 1910. But when MPs rejected this measure, the protests turned to violence. A stone was thrown through the Prime Minister's window and this was followed by groups of women breaking shop windows throughout central London. However, not all Suffragettes took part in militant tactics. Some women belonged to both the NUWSS and the WSPU.

Arguments against female suffrage

Many men, especially the politicians, were not in favour of votes for women. Many women agreed with them. Look at sources C–F. They give a range of different views as to why some people did not want to give women the vote.

D A comment by the Liberal MP W R Cremer, in 1907.
At a Parliamentary Election there would be about one million more women electors and they would swamp [out-vote] the male electors whenever they chose to do so.

E Frederick Ryland, writing in *The Girl's Own* paper, in 1896.
The factory-girl class will be the most important class of women voters ... Political power in many large cities would be chiefly in the hands of young, ill educated, giddy, and often badly behaved girls.

QUESTIONS

1 Why is the cartoonist in source F opposed to women getting the vote?

2 Study sources C, D and E. Do they agree on why women should not be given the vote?

3 Do you feel that source F best supports the views of source C, D or E? Explain your answer with reference to the sources.

"WHAT'S THE DISTURBANCE IN THE MARKET-PLACE?"
"IT'S A MASS MEETING OF THE WOMEN WHO'VE CHANGED THEIR MINDS SINCE THE MORNING AND WANT TO ALTER THEIR VOTING-PAPERS."

F A cartoon from the English magazine *Punch*, 18 December 1918.

15

The Derby 1913

A *The Times*, **5 June 1913.**

She [Emily Davison] seems to have run right in front of Anmer, which Jones was riding for the King. It was impossible to avoid her. She was ridden down, the horse turned a complete somersault and fell upon his rider. That the horse was the King's was doubtless an accident, it would need almost miraculous skill or fortune to single out any particular animal as they passed a particular point... She is said to be a person well known in the Suffragist movement, to have had a card of a Suffragist association upon her, and to have had the so-called 'Suffragist colours' tied round her waist. It is further alleged that just after she had run out in front of the horse... a placard with the words 'Votes for Women' was raised by some person in the crowd.

Suffragette protests became much more violent after the government decided not to give women the vote in 1912. In 1913 the house of Lloyd George, a leading member of the government, was badly damaged by a bomb planted by Emily Davison. Although Lloyd George was not at home, the bomb did destroy four of the bedrooms in the house. However in 1913 Emily went even further with her behaviour at Epsom racecourse, where the Derby is held each year. The Derby is, along with the Grand National, the most famous horse race in Britain. Not only would there be a huge crowd watching but the event would be heavily covered in the newspapers.

B *Lloyd's Weekly News*, **8 June 1913.**

Miss Emily Wilding Davison, the suffragette who was injured on Wednesday when she flung herself in front of the King's horse during the race for the Derby, and now lies at Epsom Cottage Hospital, was yesterday afternoon reported to be sinking... The woman's relatives have been summoned, and a serious operation has been performed, without, however, giving much hope of her recovery... It was at the famous bend on the Epsom Racecourse at Tattenham Corner that Miss Emily Wilding Davison made her mad dash. Here there are double rails to keep back the press of people who congregate to see the final effort up the home straight. Hundreds witnessed the incident, which was all over in five seconds.

C A photograph of the 1913 Derby. Emily Davison, the King's horse and jockey are all lying on the ground.

D Emmeline Pankhurst, writing in her autobiography which was published in 1914.

Miss Davison went to the races at Epsom, and breaking through the barriers . . .rushed in the path of the galloping horses and caught the bridle of the King's horse, which was leading all the others. The horse fell, throwing his jockey and crushing Miss Davison in such shocking fashion that she was carried from the course in a dying condition.

E *The Emancipation of Women* by D C Brooks, a historian, writing in 1970.

Emily Wilding Davison went to the race, dodged the police on the rails at Tattenham Corner and deliberately threw herself at the last bunch of horses. Quite by chance, she fell in front of the King's horse, Anmer; the horse was brought down, dragging along the ground the jockey, Herbert Jones, whose foot caught in the stirrup.

F Evidence of Sylvia Pankhurst, writing in the 1930s.

She had concerted [planned] a Derby protest without tragedy – a mere waving of the purple-white-and-green [Suffragette colours] at Tattenham Corner, which, by its suddenness, it was hoped would stop the race. Whether from the first her purpose was more serious, or whether a final impulse altered her resolve, I know not. . .

G Mary Richardson, a Suffragette who was standing near to Emily at Tattenham Corner.

A minute before the race started she raised a paper of her own or some kind of card before her eyes. I was watching her hand. It did not seem to shake. Even when I heard the pounding of the horses' hoofs moving closer I saw she was still smiling. And suddenly she slipped under the rail and ran out into the middle of the racecourse. It was all over so quickly. Emily was under the hoofs of one of the horses and seemed to be hurled for some distance across the grass. The horse stumbled sideways and its jockey was thrown from its back. She lay very still.

But what was Emily trying to do? Was she trying to bring down the King's horse or merely trying to walk onto the course to halt the race and make a protest. Was she trying to kill herself or was her death an accident? In 1988 the contents of her handbag were examined. It was found that she had a return ticket to Epsom and her diary contained a number of appointments for the following week.

QUESTIONS

1 Study source C. What does it tell you of the events at the Derby?

2 Study sources A and D. In what ways do they agree and in what ways do they differ in their accounts of what happened?

3 Study source E. How far does it agree with the evidence of source A or source D? Use the sources to explain your answer.

4 Study sources F and G. Which of these sources do you feel is the more reliable account? Use the other sources to explain your answer.

5 'Emily Davison tried to bring down the King's horse and kill herself in order to gain maximum publicity for the Suffragette cause.' Do the sources support this interpretation? Use the sources and the text to explain your answer.

What was the Government's Reaction?

Key Issue ▷ Why were some women given the vote in 1918?

From 1905 until the outbreak of the First World War in August 1914, about 1000 women (and about 40 men) were sent to prison because of their protest actions. Most of the women were members of the WSPU. The Suffragette prisoners wanted to be regarded as political prisoners and not criminals.

A A poster produced by the WSPU.

B Mary Leigh, a Suffragette, described what it was like to be force-fed.

The sensation is most painful – the drums of the ears seem to be bursting and there is a horrible pain in the throat and breast. I have to lie on a bed, pinned down by two wardresses, one doctor stands on a chair holding the funnel end at arm's length, and the other doctor forces the other end up the nostrils. The one holding the funnel end pours the liquid down – about a pint of milk.

In 1909 Marion Wallace Dunlop was sentenced to one month's imprisonment for defacing the wall of St Stephen's Hall. She began a new tactic and went on hunger strike in protest at not being treated as a political prisoner. After a fast lasting 91 hours she was released from jail, and so other Suffragettes copied her actions. The government responded in October by introducing forcible feeding, because it felt that it could not let Suffragettes die and so become martyrs.

In 1913 the government passed the Cat and Mouse Act. This allowed the release of hunger striking Suffragettes for a few days, and their re-arrest a few days later when they had recovered. This militancy certainly gained the Suffragettes a great deal of publicity. As source F, page 21 shows, they made the front page of the most popular newspapers. However many men were horrified by the sight of women engaged in such unladylike activities. From 1911 onwards, each time parliament debated the issue of giving the vote to women there was a greater majority against giving them the vote. In other words male MPs were becoming less and less sympathetic to the cause of votes for women.

C Sylvia Pankhurst, writing in 1913.

Undoubtedly the large part taken by women during the War in all branches of social service had proved a tremendous argument for their enfranchisement [getting the vote]. Yet the memory of the old militancy, and the certainty of its recurrence if the claims of women were set aside, was a much stronger factor.

Yet in 1918 the Representation of the People Act was passed. This gave the vote to all men over the age of 21 and all women who were over the age of 30 as well as those women who were over 21 and rented or owned their own house or were married. This meant that about 8 million women would now be able to vote. However women were still not being treated in the same way as men.

The young unmarried women who had served in the munitions factories, and all the other areas where help had been needed did not get the vote. Nonetheless the act was passed with a huge majority in the House of Commons, but with a much smaller one in the House of Lords. So why were some women given the vote in 1918, when just a few years before MPs had shown they were becoming less sympathetic to giving women the vote?

One obvious difference is that between 1914 and 1918 Britain had been at war. Campaigners from both the WSPU and the NUWSS wanted women to prove their worth by helping the war effort. The London branch of the NUWSS used its organisation to train women

E 'For King and Country'. This painting was produced during the war by E F Skinner and shows women working in a munitions factory.

to take on jobs previously held by men. They set up training classes in oxyacetylene welding as well as in munitions work. But the Suffragettes were divided. The majority, led by Emmeline Pankhurst and her daughter Christabel, supported the war because it would give women a chance to prove that they were as good as men. They demanded the 'Right to Serve', so that women could play a full part in the war effort. In July 1915, 30 000 Suffragette supporters took part in a march to demand the 'Right to Serve'. Emmeline's other daughter, Sylvia, opposed this point of view. As a revolutionary socialist she believed that women should not support a government that women had not been able to vote for.

Many women seemed to agree with Emmeline's view. Thousands of women joined up as nurses in the Voluntary Aid Detachments (VADs) while others worked in factories and in other jobs (see pages 32–33). Women were able to use the war to prove that they could play a full part in the life of the country.

D A speech by the ex-Prime Minister, Asquith, made in 1917. Before the war he had been against giving the vote to women.

How could we have carried on the war without them [women]? Wherever we turn we see them doing work which three years ago we would have regarded as 'men's work'. When the war is over the question will then arise about women's labour and their function in the new order of things. I would find it impossible to withhold from [deny] women the power and the right of making their voices directly heard [by voting].

F Brian Harrison, a modern historian.

Ever since 1918 people have said it was women's war work that gave them the vote in that year. There is something odd about the fact that in 1918 the vote was denied to women under 30 who had been so prominent [important] in the munitions factories, but granted to women over 30 whose family responsibilities had largely kept them at home.

QUESTIONS

1 Study sources C and D. In what ways do they disagree about the importance of the role of women in the First World War in bringing about voting rights?

2 Why do you think that sources C and D give different views?

3 As source F comments 'Ever since 1918 people have said that it was women's war work that gave them the vote'. To what extent do these sources explain this interpretation? Use the sources and the text to explain your answer.

The Suffrage movement: an assessment

A Herbert Gladstone, a Liberal MP and the son of the former Liberal Prime Minister William Gladstone, writing to Mrs Ennis Richmond, a Suffragette, in 1909.

Honestly, I believe that... both political parties are willing and ready to co-operate for the solution of this question [votes for women]. But no one will lift a finger now because of these absurd tactics.

Key Issue — How effective were the activities of the Suffragists and the Suffragettes?

The Suffragists and the Suffragettes had adopted very different approaches to the task of achieving votes for women. Millicent Fawcett did not agree with the attention-grabbing, violent tactics of the WSPU. Despite the fact that many women belonged to both organisations, her attitude meant that the two groups did not work together to present a united case to the government. Mrs. Fawcett relied on tried and tested tactics. She recruited MPs who were sympathetic to her cause, as well as presenting petitions to parliament, as opposed to the WSPU who used a more violent approach.

B Suffragist rally, being addressed by Fawcett.

C A school history textbook, written in 1994.

During the years 1906 to 1914 the militants increasingly hit the headlines with their forceful tactics. These included heckling Cabinet Ministers, chaining themselves to the railings of government buildings, window smashing, and the destruction of anything which might be seen as symbolic of male dominance... Once in prison they continued their protest by going on hunger strike. Parliament could not long ignore what was going on, and sympathetic MPs put forward bills to give women the vote in 1907, 1908 and 1910.

D A school textbook, written in 1973.

The suffragettes' violence won them few friends. Public opinion was probably better disposed [more supportive] towards them before the militancy of 1912–13 than after.

As early as 1866 the proposal to give the vote to women had been seriously considered and many MPs had voted in support of it. Yet over 40 years later had the situation really moved on? The more militant members of the WSPU clearly thought not. The actions of the Suffragettes from 1911 onwards certainly pushed the issue to the front pages of the newspapers. But did this help gain women the vote? Or did it mean that public opinion was less sympathetic to the cause?

Only men were MPs and only men could vote, so it was male opinion that had to be convinced but did the activities of the militant Suffragettes achieve this? Or, was it rather as the *Manchester Guardian* suggests in Source H, that votes for women were inevitable. Would they have been granted sooner or later whatever tactics had been adopted?

> **E Martin Pugh, an historian, writing in 1997.**
> Though often dramatic these [attacks on property] were never on a sufficiently large scale to make the authorities back down... All this simply irritated the public without frightening the government.

> **F Front page of the *Daily Mirror*, 23 September 1912. Suffragettes who heckled Lloyd George were attacked by men.**

> **G Christabel Pankhurst, reminiscing in 1959.**
> If Mrs Fawcett and Mother had stood together at the door of the House of Commons, it might have opened. The Prime Minister could not easily have fought both wings of the Women's Movement.

> **H *Manchester Guardian*, Obituary of Millicent Fawcett, 6 August 1929.**
> There were three stages in the emancipation of women. The first was the long campaign of propaganda and organisation, at the centre of which, always hopefully, stood Dame Millicent Fawcett. The second was the campaign of the militants, which, since it depended on sensation, brought to the movement the enthusiastic attention of the popular press and made it a live political issue. The third was the war. Had there been no militancy and no war, the emancipation of women would still have come, although more slowly.

QUESTIONS

1 Study source B. What does it tell you about Suffragist tactics?

2 Study sources A and F. To what extent do they agree about the effects of suffragette tactics?

3 Study sources A and C. In what ways do they agree about the effects of suffragette tactics?

4 How can you explain the difference in attitudes between sources A and C?

5 'The militant tactics of the Suffragettes slowed down the process of women gaining the vote.' How do the sources and text support this interpretation?

5 | The Impact of the First World War

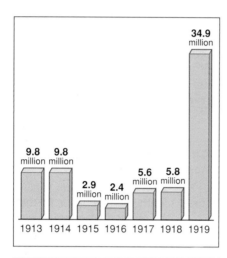

A Men queuing outside Lambeth Town Hall in order to join the army.

B Working days lost through strikes. This means that the number of workers on strike is multiplied by the number of days on strike. Therefore 9 million working days could mean 9 million workers on strike for one day or it could mean 1 million workers on strike for nine days.

C 'A striking contrast.' This cartoon comes from the Christmas 1918 edition of *The Dump* – a newspaper produced once a year by troops in France.

How did the government tackle the demands of war?

In the nineteenth century the Liberals and the Conservatives had generally agreed that the government should not get involved with the day-to-day lives of ordinary people. However, at the beginning of the twentieth century the Liberal reforms had begun to increase the role of the government. The First World War accelerated this trend. Suddenly the government was forced to take charge of large parts of daily life. Five million men were ordered into the army, the publication of news was controlled, even the time on the clock was changed. However this was not the government's intention at the start of the war. They, like most other people, expected the war to be over quickly.

The early months

In the early months the government thought that they had enough ammunition and supplies. The Chancellor of the Exchequer, Lloyd George, promised that Britain's businesses would be able to 'carry on business as usual.' How wrong he was. The war used up men and supplies at an unbelievable rate. The government unintentionally made matters worse because its campaign to get men to volunteer to join the army was so successful.

All over the country skilled men in important jobs were leaving to go and fight. The result was that production fell just when it needed to increase. Miners were needed down the coal mines and farmers were needed to grow crops but many of them were volunteering to join the army. To make matters even worse these men were then killed in huge numbers and so had to be replaced by yet more men. Britain could not continue to fight the war in such an uncontrolled way. Gradually the government took control of more and more aspects of people's lives.

Conscription

By 1916 the number of men volunteering was far less than in the early stages of the war. It was now obvious that there would be no quick victory. The large lists of casualties being published in newspapers meant that people began to realise that this war was very different to previous wars. Therefore, for the first time ever, a British government introduced **conscription**. Men were ordered to fight in the war. The Military Service Act of January 1916 called up all unmarried men between the ages of 18 and 41. In May 1916 this was extended to cover all married men as well.

However, conscription was not introduced simply to make sure there were enough soldiers to replace those who had been killed. It meant that the government could also try to ensure that workers who were in important jobs did not join the army. Workers in essential industries were not conscripted. This meant people such as miners, train drivers and munitions workers. However, the government still allowed these men to volunteer, so the shortages continued.

The workforce

The government needed to replace the skilled workers who were going off to fight in the war. A particular problem was that in many industries skilled work could only be done by workers who had received many years of training. These skilled workers received higher wages. However there was no longer enough time to give workers years of training. The government therefore wanted to introduce **dilution**. This meant that unskilled or semi-skilled workers with basic training could carry out skilled work.

In March 1915 Lloyd George arranged a conference with the leaders of the trade unions. The result of this conference was the Treasury Agreement. The unions agreed to allow dilution. However, Lloyd George had to promise that this would end once the war was over. Also he had to agree that these new workers would be paid the same as skilled workers. This was because the unions were afraid that the government was introducing dilution just to reduce workers' wages.

The Treasury Agreement was followed by the Munitions of War Act in July 1915. This banned workers in the munitions industry from going on strike. It also introduced the leaving certificate. It meant that no worker could leave his job without the permission of his employer. This was to make sure that factories were not short of essential workers but it also meant that workers could not leave to get a better job. If they did leave without a certificate they had to wait six weeks before they could start a new job. Few workers could survive without six weeks' wages and so the certificate was hated.

D Lloyd George, speaking in June 1915.

We must appeal to the patriotism of the unions to relax these particular rules. . . to enable us to turn out the necessary munitions of war to win a real and speedy triumph.

E AJ Cook, a miners' leader. April 1916.

The chains of slavery are being welded ever tighter upon us. . .An industrial truce was entered into by our leaders behind our backs. . . Away with the industrial truce! We must not stand by and allow the workers to be exploited and our liberties taken away.

QUESTIONS

1 Why was the government so concerned about the munitions industry?

2 Study source C. What is the cartoonist's opinion of the workers back in Britain?

3 Study source B. How useful is this source in supporting the point made by source C?

4 How useful is source C to a historian studying the attitudes of the British people to the war?

5 Study sources D and E. Why do you think they give different views about how the workers should behave during the war?

6 'The British people enthusiastically supported government measures to win the war.' Using your own knowledge and the sources, explain whether you agree with this interpretation.

Defence expenditure

1913	£91m
1918	£1956

Artillery pieces

1914	91
1918	8039

Machine guns

1914	300
1918	120 900

A British annual expenditure and production figures.

During the war the government took control of those industries which were most important to winning the war such as steel production, shipbuilding, mining and the railways. This ensured that raw materials, food and vital supplies got to where they were needed, and that factories had enough power. This started in 1915 when Lloyd George became the first ever Minister of Munitions. Earlier that year there had been a scandal because the generals claimed that the British army did not have enough artillery shells to fight the Germans. Lloyd George was determined to increase munitions production. He used his powers to introduce dilution as a result of the Treasury Agreement (see page 23).

The main effect of Lloyd George's changes was that almost 1 million women were employed in the munitions industry by 1918. Also 20 000 new munitions factories had been set up. By 1918 Britain was actually managing to produce enough weapons and ammunition for its army of 4 million men. Lloyd George also ordered far more machine guns than the generals requested. He realised that they were the key weapon in trench warfare. Britain began the war with just 1330 machine guns but ended it with 240 000.

Lloyd George was so successful that in December 1916 he became Prime Minister. The government had realised that it had to get directly involved to make sure enough munitions were produced. After the success over munitions the government also got involved in other essential industries. For instance, the railways were taken over. At the start of the war there were 130 railway companies running the system. During the war it was run by the managers from the ten largest companies and profits were shared out. A

B How the workforce changed. Figures are in thousands.

C *Morning Post* **14 March 1916.**

At Southampton yesterday Robert Andrew Smith was fined for treating his wife to a glass of wine in a local public-house. He said his wife gave him sixpence to pay for her drink. Mrs Smith was also fined £1 for consuming and Dorothy Brown, the barmaid, £5 for selling the intoxicant, contrary to the regulations of the Liquor Control Board.

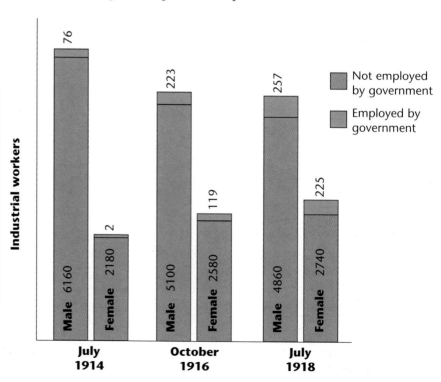

Industrial workers

Not employed by government

Employed by government

July 1914 — Male 6160, 76 — Female 2180, 2

October 1916 — Male 5100, 223 — Female 2580, 119

July 1918 — Male 4860, 257 — Female 2740, 225

centrally run railway system meant that troops and munitions could be moved rapidly to wherever they were needed. The government also bought essential raw materials to make sure there were no shortages. For instance in 1916 the government bought the entire Indian jute crop. Jute was used to produce the sandbags for the trenches.

The Defence of the Realm Acts

The Defence of the Realm Acts (DORA) were a series of measures designed to give the government control over many aspects of life. The first of them was passed in 1914. One of the Acts cut down the length of time that pubs could open. Before the war pubs were allowed to open from early morning and so workers sometimes arrived at work already drunk. Now pubs were usually limited to opening from midday to 2.30 p.m. and from 6.30 to 9.30 in the evening. Drunkenness meant that workers didn't work so hard, and it could be a real danger in the munitions industry. Beer was also watered down to make it less alcoholic and the price of beer was raised to make it too expensive to get drunk. It was also illegal to buy drinks (called 'treating') for other people – even your wife! (See source C.)

'British Summer Time' was also introduced. The government ordered that clocks should be put forward. This was done to create an extra hour of daylight so that workers, particularly on farms, could work for longer. Newspapers were **censored** so that their reports of battles did not give vital information to the Germans. Soldiers' letters home to their families were also censored. Lighting Regulations were introduced. Street lights were masked as part of a blackout so that German Zeppelins and bombers would not be able to see British towns. Shop windows and advertisements could not be lit, so that coal was not wasted producing electricity for non-essential purposes.

Financing the war

Fighting a war on such a scale was extremely expensive. It has been estimated that the war cost £9 billion. The government increased income tax from just 1 shilling 2d (less than 6p) in the pound in 1914 to 6 shillings (30p) in the pound. How times had changed. In 1909 the House of Lords had been upset that the rich were to pay just 2.5 per cent more in tax. Not only was the tax rate increased but so was the number of people who paid it. At the start of the war only the richest 1 million people paid income tax. By the end of the war 3 million people were paying tax. Death duties were also increased as was the tax on profits in a range of industries.

However tax alone could not produce enough money for the government. Free trade was also sacrificed as import duties were introduced on luxury goods such as cars and clocks. However the war was mainly paid for by increasing the national debt. Huge amounts of money were borrowed, mainly from the United States. By the end of the war Britain owed £7.4 billion and this would have to be paid back, with interest. Ordinary people were encouraged to help by lending money to the government in the form of buying war savings certificates (see source D).

D Buy War Savings Certificates. People were encouraged to lend the government money which would be paid back once the war was over.

QUESTIONS

1 Study source A. What is the link between source A and the huge increase in income tax during the war?

2 Study source B.
a) How many men were working in government-run industries at the beginning of the war?
b) How many men were working in these industries by July 1918?
c) How can you explain these figures?

3 What does source C tell you about how regulations were enforced during the war?

4 Study source D. Why was this poster published during the war?

5 'Victory was achieved in 1918 but the loss of individual freedom was too high a price to pay.' Use the sources and your own knowledge to explain:
a) how this interpretation was reached; and
b) whether you agree or disagree with it.

The Impact of War on Civilians

Key Issue How were civilians affected by the war?

During past European wars, people in Britain had been protected from the day-to-day effects. Cities in Europe might be burnt to the ground and people might die of starvation as crops were destroyed, but the British people were safe on their island. The First World War would be different. For the first time civilians would find that the war could be brought to their own front door. Food became increasingly scarce as the war went on. Also, for the first time ever, British people were attacked by bombs falling from the sky.

Food

Before the war Britain had imported large amounts of food. Bread was the basic food for a large percentage of the population but most of the wheat came from distant countries like Canada. In 1915 the Germans decided to try and starve the British into defeat by attacking merchant shipping bringing supplies into the country. Their weapon was the submarine or U-boat.

In 1915 the Germans had only 21 U-boats but as they built more they became very successful. By the end of the war they had sunk 11 million tons of merchant shipping. In April 1917 Britain had just six weeks of grain left, and starvation threatened. However the navy, by using convoys of merchant ships protected by destroyers, overcame the U-boat threat and food imports once more kept Britain alive.

It was just as well that Britain was able to import food because food production in Britain initially declined. Many farm workers volunteered to join the army while factories which had once produced farm machinery were converted to the production of military vehicles. The result was food shortages and queues at shops.

Food shortages created a real problem for the government. Prices shot up. If people could not afford to buy food they were likely to strike for higher wages. In 1917 the government decided to control the price of grain for bread. A similar arrangement was introduced for potatoes. In effect a maximum price was introduced for both bread and potatoes. The government gave money to farmers so that they did not make a loss at these prices. People were encouraged to eat less bread. In 1916 the King issued a proclamation asking people to eat 25 per cent less bread and not to use flour in other cooking.

However the fear of lack of food led to panic buying, which of course produced shortages in the shops. Therefore in January 1918, the Ministry of Food decided to introduce rationing. Sugar was the first item to be rationed and this was followed later by butchers' meat. Rationing was first introduced in London and the south east. In July it was extended to the rest of the country.

C Food shortages were common, with shops often running out of stocks of some food.

> **D** Elsie McIntyre recalls life during the war.
> The most awful thing was food. It was very scarce. And as we were coming off shift someone would say 'There is a bit of steak at the butchers'. . . [so] you went straight into a queue.

E A government poster to encourage people to eat less bread. Wheat imports had to get past the German U-boats.

Britain really was the 'home front'. Rationing meant that everyone was making a sacrifice. Basic foods like meat, bread, sugar, butter and margarine could only be bought with a ration card in fixed amounts. The amount of food you could buy depended on your job. People in manual work got more food than those who were in office jobs. Teenage boys got more than girls.

The Woman's Land Army

The government needed more workers producing food, but the terrible casualties on the Western Front meant that all available men were needed in the army. In 1915 the Board of Education allowed children to miss school to work on farms. The Women's Land Army (WLA) was also set up. Its purpose was to encourage women to work on farms and replace the men who had gone to fight in the war. Some farmers resisted this measure and in 1916 the Board of Trade began sending officials around the country in an effort to persuade farmers to accept women workers. The WLA had a less glamorous image than the armed services when they were created and so only 48 000 women joined.

F Women's Land Army. A poster to try and encourage women to join up by making the work seem attractive. However the problem often lay with the farmers who didn't want to employ women on their farms.

QUESTIONS

1 Study sources A and B. Do they agree on people's reaction to the food situation?

2 Study sources C and E. Do you think they are equally useful to a historian studying how civilians were affected by the war?

3 Study source D. Does it back up the view of the war given in source C or source E?

4 'Britain came close to defeat on the Home Front during the war.' How far do the sources and text support this interpretation?

In the Front Line

Because so many men were needed to fight in the war, the building industry almost came to a complete standstill. Working-class housing was already in a terrible state, as the work of people like Seebohm Rowntree had shown (see page 9). Four years of war meant that the situation became even worse. No new houses could be built and so housing shortages developed in industrial areas as people left the country and came to work in factories. This resulted in serious overcrowding and diseases, such as tuberculosis and bronchitis, rose dramatically.

However, in contrast, many people's diet actually improved. This was because the amount of sugar and butter that people consumed was much reduced. Also meat was often in short supply so people ate more fish. Less alcohol was drunk both because of the DORA regulations and the fact that grain was needed to make bread. The limit on pub opening hours wasn't abolished until 1989. It was only meant to last until the end of the First World War! Also there was more nutrition in the bread since vital energy could not be wasted on refining bread, so wholewheat bread was eaten rather than refined white bread.

Another major change for the British people was that they were brought into the front line of the war. On 16 December 1914 German naval ships bombarded Scarborough and Hartlepool and over 100 people were killed or injured. This was soon followed by attacks from the air. On 19 January 1915 the first Zeppelin raid took place. Zeppelins were giant airships which were filled with hydrogen. They could fly higher than the aircraft of the time and so seemed invulnerable as they silently glided across English skies.

In 1915 there were 20 Zeppelin raids in Britain which killed 188 people. During the entire war bombs dropped by Zeppelins caused 564 deaths. However, on 3 September 1916 Lieutenant Leefe Robinson managed to get his plane up to a Zeppelin and shot it down. He was immediately awarded the Victoria Cross. After that other fighter planes were able to repeat his attack and the Zeppelins became less of a threat.

In 1917 the Germans started to use a new tactic. The long-distance bomber aeroplane was introduced. This could carry a much heavier bomb than the Zeppelin. On 13 June 1917 162 people were killed and a further 432 injured in a single raid on London. The government reacted by introducing a blackout throughout the country. There were no street lights at night. Factories were ordered to stop work if Zeppelins or bombers were spotted nearby.

A A recruitment poster showing a Zeppelin flying over St Paul's Cathedral in London.

B Soldiers of the Territorial Army clear up after a Zeppelin bombing raid on King's Lynn in Norfolk on 19 January 1915.

C Tom Morgan recalls the effect of a Zeppelin raid, as told to him by his grandmother, Florence Hill.

On January 31st, 1916, nine airships left their bases in Germany in order to bomb Liverpool. However Zeppelin L21 got lost and accidentally bombed Wednesbury, the village where Florence lived, believing it to be Liverpool.

Dietrich's bombing run began. Bombs fell on Tipton and Bradley and then the first bombs fell on Wednesbury. They landed in the King Street area, near to a large factory. A woman, Mrs Smith, of 14, King Street, left her house to see what the noise was. A little way down the street she saw fires and presumed an explosion at the factory. She walked towards the fires but bombs began to fall behind her. She turned and hurried home, to find her house demolished and all her family killed – her husband Joseph, daughter Nellie aged 13, son Thomas, 11. Three bodies were quickly located. The youngest girl Ina, just seven, was lying dead on the roof of the factory. Her body would not be found until the morning. The first Wednesbury deaths had occurred. Above, L21 hovered, barely moving for the moment.

D Winifred Tower kept a diary during the war. Here she comments on how fear of raids by Zeppelins had changed London.

In Princes Gate every other lamp was lighted and in many places only every 3rd or 4th. All illuminated shop signs were forbidden, also bright head-lights on motor cars etc. Blinds had to be pulled down as soon as lights were lit . . . Most people had water or buckets of sand or fire extinguishers on every landing. We rather laughed at this at first but by degrees everyone came round to taking certain precautions.

E Mr Ernest Cooper, the Town Clerk of Southwold in Suffolk, describes the shooting down of a Zeppelin in his diary, 25 January 1917.

At 3.30 [at night] there was a big burst of flame in the sky over Southwold House and we saw it was a Zeppelin alight. She soon broke in two and then began to descend in a wavy line, roaring flames at the head and a long tail of sparks and smoke far up behind. She came down very slowly at first and I had a good view with my glasses [binoculars] . . . It was a great sight and the people who were out all cheered and those who were in bed came running out in their night dresses . . . The Capt. of the Zepp and two men landed alive which seems almost incredible but we hear one died afterwards. I think 17 were killed.

QUESTIONS

1 Study source B. What does it tell you about the effects of Zeppelin raids on Britain?

2 Study source C. How far does it support the view of Zeppelin raids given in source B?

3 Which do you think is the more reliable account, source B or source C? Use the sources to explain your answer.

4 Study source E. To what extent does it give a different view of Zeppelin raids to that in Sources B and C?

5 Why do you think it gives a different view?

6 'The British people were frightened by the Zeppelin attacks'. How far do the sources support this interpretation?

Women's work before the outbreak of the war

At the beginning of the century most women did not have paid work. The government **census** of 1911 revealed that over 11 million adult women did not have a paid job, in contrast to fewer than 5 million women who did. The reason for this was that women were expected to marry and become housewives. Their job was to care for their husbands and bring up a family. Women grew up accepting that men earned the money for the family. Women were dependent upon men. They grew up in a household dominated by men, and then they left to get married, once more to be dominated by the man.

A Housekeeper with the female servants or 'slaveys', 1895.

For working-class women, the commonest jobs were as servants and cooks. This was known as 'going into service'. Although some servants were married, service was considered to be especially suitable for a young woman because it taught her the skills that she would need to be a housewife. In other words, even working-class husbands expected their wives to give up their jobs once they were married. Many men did not consider it to be respectable to send their wives out to work. Even though it meant the family having to survive on little money, this was considered to be better than having a wife who worked. However, some working-class women did not have a choice about working. Their husbands did not earn enough and so wives had to have a paid job as well as being a housewife.

In the industrial areas of Britain in the north and the midlands many women worked in factories. Once more, the majority of those who worked were unmarried women, although married women were allowed to work in factories. The Lancashire textile mills were famous for employing large numbers of women. Indeed the percentage of Lancashire working-class women with a job was about the same in 1900 as it is today. Throughout the country many poor women also worked in what were known as the 'sweated' trades, such as hat and dress-making. They were forced to work long hours for little money. Even so, the majority of working-class women didn't have a job. Those who did were paid far less than men.

Middle-class girls might work as shop assistants or in an office, but they were expected to give up the job as soon as they got married. Indeed some jobs, such as teaching and bank work, demanded this. However, women were paid much less than men, even when they were doing similar work.

Although the life of a middle-class woman did not include a job

B An advertisement for Coca-Cola, 1900.

it had many benefits. Her house would have been full of servants to do the cooking and the cleaning. This left women with a great deal of time to do other things, such as play tennis or visit friends. A wife and daughters with lots of time on their hands was a sign of status for a middle-class family. Things were not the same for working-class wives. Even those who had a job still had to feed the family and keep the house clean despite having little money. Cleanliness was seen as a sign of respectability. The front step of the house was kept spotlessly clean as an outward sign of this.

By 1900 boys and girls received a similar basic schooling. However, far more boys than girls were likely to go on to secondary school. Just a very few rich girls went to university. In the 1850s Millicent Fawcett's sister, Elizabeth Garrett Anderson, had been refused the chance to become a medical student. Although her example eventually led to women training to be doctors, there were still only 260 in the whole of Britain in 1900.

C Enid Starkie, writing in 1941, remembers her childhood at the turn of the century.

My father seemed to me to be a very important person ... In my mother's opinion everything he did was right ... She considered it right that the life of a wife, that the life of all women in the household, should revolve around its male head. Nurse, the maids and even Lizzie the cook, accepted this attitude without question.

D Katherine Chorley, writing about her life at the start of the twentieth century.

My schooling should lead up to a few years of life at home before, if all went well, I got suitably married, my days being filled by golf and tennis with other social activities, some charity work — that was important – and some reading and perhaps a little art.

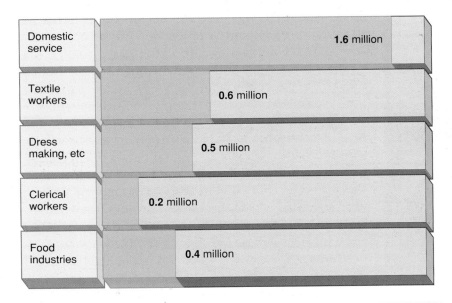

Domestic service	1.6 million
Textile workers	0.6 million
Dress making, etc	0.5 million
Clerical workers	0.2 million
Food industries	0.4 million

E The numbers of women employed in the most common occupations for women in 1911.

QUESTIONS

1 Study source E. Which was the most common job for women in 1911?

2 Why was this? Use the text to explain your answer.

3 Study source D. What social class do you think Katherine Chorley came from? Give reasons for your answer.

4 Study sources B and D. Which source is the more useful to the historian studying the life of women at the beginning of the twentieth century?

5 'All women were discriminated against at the beginning of the twentieth century, but working-class women suffered the most.' How far do the sources and text support this interpretation?

Women and the War

A A poster to encourage women to join the VADs.

The war offered many women great opportunities for work. This could either be direct involvement, such as becoming a nurse or joining one of the women's services, or it could involve taking over the jobs of the men who had gone to fight. In 1915 the Marchioness of Londonderry set up the Women's Legion, which organised more than 40 000 women to work as cooks and nurses in the army and so allow more men to go and fight. The Voluntary Aid Detachments (VADs) had been set up in 1910 to provide more nurses for the army. They were open to both men and women but in the event it was mainly women who joined up, with over 15 000 volunteering during the war.

There was no pay and so only women from reasonably well-off families could join the VADs. Many of them had little idea of what awaited them. Vera Brittain, who served in the VADs, remarked that women 'came to the hospital expecting to hold the patients' hands and smooth their pillows while regular nurses fetched and carried everything that looked and smelt disagreeable'. The reality was very different. Even though the VADs were stationed well behind the front lines, they had to work long hours and look after men who were in constant pain and suffering from terrible wounds.

However, for many middle and upper-class women the VADs provided the first ever opportunity to leave home and become independent people. In the main, working-class women had to seek their opportunities for war work on the home front (see pages 34–35). The first

B A VAD motor driver. Painting by Gilbert Rogers, an official artist. His job was to paint an accurate record of the war.

VAD unit left for France in October 1914. But the VADs were not only nurses. In 1915 the scheme was extended by the creation of the VAD General Section. This organised women to carry out jobs such as cooks, clerks and accountants. The idea was to free men from these jobs so that they could fight in the front line. It also provided an opportunity for those women who didn't want to become nurses.

The Two Madonnas of Pervyse

For some women even the VADs were not enough. Elsie Knocker and Mairi Chisholm had gone to Belgium to work as nurses in a hospital but had realised that many men with non-critical injuries were dying of shock long before they reached the hospital. Therefore the two women set up their own first aid post right behind the front lines in the Belgian town of Pervyse. For three and a half years they tended the wounded, until they were caught up in a German gas attack and had to be sent back to England. They were named the Two Madonnas of Pervyse by the local people, and they were awarded the Military Medal by the British army.

Although women could join the VADs and do various jobs, until 1917 they couldn't actually join the armed forces. In the first days of the war a voluntary organisation, the Women's Emergency Reserve, had been formed. This later changed its name to the Women's Volunteer Reserve. It provided volunteers to run canteens and ambulances for the troops, as well as raising money to provide facilities for them. However, although it had a uniform it was not an official group. The armed forces were not considered to be a place for women.

This view began to change with the terrible casualties being suffered, especially after the Battle of the Somme. In 1917 all three services set up women's sections: the Women's Army Auxiliary Corps (WAAC), the Women's Royal Naval Service (WRNS) and the Women's Royal Air Force (WRAF). These sections employed over 10 000 women as drivers, typists and cooks. The army needed to send every possible fighting man to the front, and having women carrying out the non-combatant jobs allowed them to do this.

C Mairi Chisholm describes what it was like being a front line nurse, in an oral interview in 1976.

We slept with our clothes on – at any moment you'd hear a roar of 'blessés, blessés, blessés' [wounded men] and the door would be flung open and the soldiers would bring in one of their companions. And also we went out into the trenches a lot ourselves, and poked our noses around to see everybody was all right, and occasionally we went out into the advance trenches, which were within 25 yards of the Germans.

D The girl behind the man behind the gun. A government poster to encourage women to join the Queen Mary's Auxiliary Corps.

E A book produced by the government in 1918 describes the purpose of the WAACs.

Each cook replaces one man, while among the clerks at present the ratio is four women to three men. Every WAAC who goes to France is like the pawn who attains the top of the chessboard and is exchanged for a more valuable piece. She sends a fighting man to his job by taking all the jobs that are really a woman's after all. For is it not woman's earliest job to look after man?

QUESTIONS

1 Study source A. Why was this poster published? Use the source and the text to explain your answer.

2 Do you think source A or source B is more useful to the historian studying the role of women in the war?

3 Study source D. What image of women is presented in this poster?

4 'Women in the First World War were still second-class citizens.' Use the sources and text to explain whether or not you agree with this interpretation.

The Right to Serve

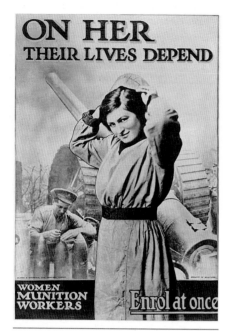

ON HER
THEIR LIVES DEPEND

WOMEN MUNITION WORKERS

Enrol at once

A A government poster to encourage women to become workers in munitions factories.

In July 1915 Christabel Pankhurst led a march of 30 000 women who demanded 'The Right to Serve'. This was soon granted. In January 1916 conscription was introduced. No longer could the army rely on volunteers. Men would be ordered to join up. This meant that there was a need for women to fill the jobs which were being left by the men. Quite often these were jobs which had never been done by women. Women became conductors on buses and trams, though very few were allowed to become drivers. Drivers were paid more than conductors. Men were worried that if women became drivers it would cause their wages to be reduced.

Women were also allowed to join the police force for the first time. They became chimney sweeps and ran bakeries. As early as 1916 every London ambulance was driven by a woman. Nearly 750 000 women took jobs as clerks, and while this type of job had been filled by women before the war, they had never done so in such huge numbers.

Canaries

Not every job filled by a woman was as a replacement for a man. In 1915 the army blamed its defeats on a lack of artillery shells. The British people were horrified to think that soldiers might be dying simply because the government was not doing its job properly. The result of this was a huge increase in the production of shells by private companies. New jobs were created in these munitions factories, and by the end of the war over 900 000 women had filled them.

However, this was very dangerous work. Explosions could kill and maim the workers. The chemicals used in the explosives caused workers to vomit and eventually turned their skin yellow, earning

B Caroline Rennles, a canary in the war, remembers how she felt.

Sometimes the trains were packed, so of course the porters knew that we were all munitions kids, and they'd say, 'Go on girl, 'op in there', and they would open the first class carriages ... Of course conductors used to say on the trains 'you'll die in two years, cock.' So we said, 'We don't mind dying for our country.' We were so young we didn't realise.

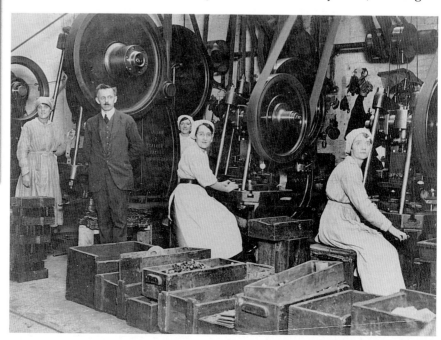

C Women workers at a Manchester munitions factory, along with their male supervisor.

them the nickname of canaries. The chemicals sometimes caused cancer and infertility.

Nevertheless, munitions work was very well paid, often twice as much as working as a servant. In some cases a munitions worker could earn as much as £5 a week. Therefore many working-class women were willing to do this work.

Greater freedoms for women

Before the war, unmarried middle and upper-class girls would always have been chaperoned – usually by an older female relative. The war gave much greater freedom to women, especially single women. By going out to work they could now meet men on their own. This freedom changed some attitudes. It was now more acceptable for women to smoke and drink in public. The war also saw a great increase in illegitimate births. Any girl who had a baby outside marriage was considered to be immoral. At a time when birth control was not available to ordinary people many girls were forced to have illegal abortions. Some died from these.

> **E An article from the *Illustrated London News*, 13 January 1917.**
> There is a good deal of criticism of women 'shop-gazing' in the towns, especially in the West End of London. It is really the most inexpensive of activities. . . . but it is said, those women round the shop windows are wasting time in which they might be making munitions, or setting free others – their servants and needlewomen – to go and make munitions. We must remember that the majority of the 'shop-gazing' women are probably workers in the home. The work of women in the home is indispensable and genuine.

F The change in the number of women in paid work.

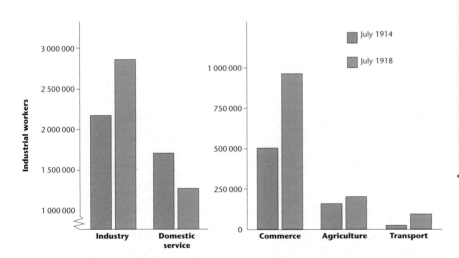

> **D Gabrielle West describes conditions in a munitions factory in 1917.**
> The change rooms were fearfully crowded, long troughs were provided instead of wash basins, and there is always a scarcity of soap and towels. The girls' danger clothes are often horribly dirty and in rags . . . Although the fumes often meant 16 or 18 casualties a night there were only four beds for men and women and they are all in the same room.

QUESTIONS

1 Study source A. What message does it give?

2 Study source C. In what way does it give a different message?

3 Study sources A and C. Do you think source A or source C gives the more reliable picture of life in a munitions factory?

4 Study source D. Why do you think it gives a different view of life in a munitions factory from that shown in source A?

5 Study source F. Only domestic service shows a drop in numbers. How can you explain this?

6 Study sources E and F. How far do these sources agree or disagree about the lives of women during the war?

Why did so many men volunteer to fight in the First World War?

At midnight on 4 August 1914 Britain declared war on Germany. When the war began Britain had an army of only 100 000 men. This army was immediately sent to France as the British Expeditionary Force (BEF). But as the two sides dug in along the Western Front, vast numbers of soldiers were required to try and drive the German army out of France and Belgium. The British government needed men to join the army. Posters were one way of achieving this.

Lord Kitchener became the new Minister of War and he asked for men to enlist. They did so in huge numbers. By the end of the first week 175 000 had volunteered and by the end of the first month this figure had increased to 750 000. In total 2.5 million men volunteered to fight.

Why did so many men join up?

Many people joined up out of patriotism, because their king and country had asked them. Kitchener was the popular face of the country and his finger pointed from countless posters. People believed that it was Britain's moral duty to defend Belgium from the German 'bullies'. As Rupert Brooke wrote: 'Now God be thanked who has matched us with His hour'. British people believed that God and Britain were on the same side.

People were encouraged to believe that the war would soon be over. The popular view was that it would be 'over by Christmas'.

A A government recruiting poster.

C At the Front. A government recruiting poster.

D Germany means to starve us out. A government recruiting poster.

B Kitchener's face stares out from this recruitment poster.

E Rifleman Bernard Britland was one of those who volunteered in September 1914. In January 1915 he wrote this letter to his family.

The Sergeant-Major was so [impressed] with the progress we made that he served 25 rifles out to the smartest of us. I was one of the 25 so you can bet I didn't half feel proud of myself. The draft that was here before us were two or three weeks before they got their rifles and we had them in three days so that is something to be proud of isn't it?

We are being well fed here. This morning we had a tin of sardines each for breakfast . . . For dinner we generally have potatoes, haricot beans, roast meat, stewed meat, cabbage and green peas so there is plenty of variety.

F A British soldier describes how he felt after volunteering.

I went home each evening with my rifle on my shoulder . . . Girls smiled at me, men looked at me with respect, the bus drivers wished me luck and refused to take my money for my fare.

There would be a quick, glorious victory followed by a hero's return. Few people imagined the horrors ahead. Besides, for many young men life contained little adventure. They had left school and gone to work in their local town. Few could afford holidays. The war provided an opportunity to break out of this dull life. The posters promised a world of adventure and excitement. When the war was over they would be treated as heroes.

Another reason for joining up was that many working-class people in Britain were very poor. Large numbers worked in industries, which regularly laid them off without pay when there was little work. The army offered them a regular wage and regular meals.

Posters were used to make those who had not joined up feel guilty. In particular women were encouraged to convince their husbands and boyfriends to join up. Others were persuaded to enlist by the idea of Pals' Battalions. Friends from a local area were encouraged to join up together. Sometimes people who worked together joined up together. Sometimes it was men who played together in a local team. As friends trained and fought together they would help to keep each other's spirits up, and give each other courage. But the problem with this became clear once these Pals' Battalions became involved in heavy fighting. Then whole groups of men from the same town or village died together. The effect on the local community could be devastating.

G Lionel Ferguson recalled his reasons for joining up in an interview in 1978.

That afternoon I decided to join the Liverpool Scottish. What sights I saw on my way up to Frazer Street: a queue of men over two miles long in the Haymarket; the recruiting office took over a week to pass in all those thousands. At the Liverpool Scottish HQ things seemed hopeless; in fact I was giving up hopes of ever getting in, when I saw Rennison, an officer of the battalion, and he invited me into the mess, getting me in front of hundreds of others. I counted myself in luck to secure the last kilt, which although very old and dirty, I carried away to tog myself in.

H George Coppard was just 16 when he volunteered in 1914.

I knew I had to enlist straight away. I presented myself to the recruiting sergeant at Mitcham Road Barracks, Croydon. There was a steady stream of men, mostly working types, queuing to enlist. The sergeant asked me my age, and when told, replied, "Clear off son. Come back tomorrow and see if you're nineteen, eh?" So I turned up again the next day and gave my age as nineteen. I attested [took the oath] in a batch of a dozen others and, holding up my right hand, swore to fight for King and Country. The sergeant winked as he gave me the King's shilling, plus one shilling and ninepence (8½p) ration money for that day.

QUESTIONS

1 Study sources A and B. Which emotion are they trying to appeal to?

2 Study sources E and F. What other reasons for joining up are suggested by these two soldiers?

3 Study sources C and D. Which source do you think Rifleman Britland (source E) would be impressed by?

4 Study sources G and H. Do they provide useful evidence to the historian studying the effects of government propaganda?

Censorship and Propaganda

A The Times 27 August 1914.

Nearly all the people I interrogated had stories to tell of German atrocities. Whole villages, they said, had been put to fire and sword. One man, whom I did not see, told an official of the Catholic Society that he had seen with his own eyes Germans chop off the arms of a baby which clung to its mother's skirts.

C Irving Cobb, an American reporter who was in Belgium when the Germans invaded.

Every Belgian refugee had a tale to tell of German atrocities on non-combatants: but not once did we find an avowed [genuine] eye-witness to such things. Always our informant had heard of the torturing or the maiming or the murdering, but never had he personally seen it. It had always happened in another town – never in his own town.

D In his book *Eyewitness*, Ernest Swinton, explained how he carried out his work as the official reporter on the war.

The principle which guided me in my work was above all to avoid helping the enemy. This appeared to me even more important than the purveyance of news to our own people. For home consumption – that is for those who were carrying the burden and footing the bill – I decided to tell as much of the truth as was compatible with safety, to guard against depression and pessimism, and to check unjustified optimism which might lead to a relaxation of effort.

Key Issue How effective was government propaganda during the war?

Issuing posters to try to get men to join the army was one sort of **propaganda**. However the British government used propaganda techniques for other purposes. In particular the government did not want British civilians to feel like giving up because the war wasn't worth it. Keeping up civilian morale was a significant aim of the government.

B Part of the Bryce Report on Alleged German Atrocities.

One witness saw a German soldier cut a woman's breasts after he had murdered her, and saw many other dead bodies of women in the streets of Belgium. Another witness testified that she saw a drunken German soldier kill a two-year-old child: The soldier drove his bayonet with both hands into the child's stomach, lifting the child into the air on his bayonet, he and his comrades were singing. Other witnesses saw a German soldier amputate a child's hands and feet.

Censorship and the War Office Press Bureau

Civilians wanted to know what was happening in the war. They would want to read about it in the newspapers. However this presented the government with a problem. It obviously did not want the enemy to find out about British troop movements by reading the newspapers! But also the government was aware that if civilians read about the true horror of the war morale might fall. Therefore in 1914 the government set up the War Office Press Bureau. Its job was to censor news from the front and then issue reports to the press. At first only one British officer, Ernest Swinton, was allowed to cover the war from the front and all the newspapers had to use his reports.

However in 1915 this policy was changed. Newspaper journalists from the major British newspapers became accredited, that is they were allowed to go to the front and write reports. However everything they wrote still had to be submitted to a government censor. It was not just newspaper reports that were censored. Even the letters from soldiers to their families were checked.

Film

However, censored newspaper reports were not enough for a public who simply could not get enough information about the war. Therefore in August 1916 cinemas across Britain were screening *The Battle of the Somme*, a film lasting over an hour and showing scenes from the battle which had begun on 1 July and which would last

E Two scenes from the Battle of the Somme.
a The men go over the top. This scene was almost certainly a reconstruction, made days after the actual attack.
b A genuine moment from the battle. The soldier on this man's back died just 30 minutes later.

until November. In other words the public in Britain could watch a battle that was still continuing across the English Channel. It drew huge audiences. However, the actual battle scenes were probably reconstructed and it was of course a silent film. But it achieved its aim of showing the public the British army in action.

The War Propaganda Bureau

The government did not stop at such innocent ways of improving the morale of civilians. The War Propaganda Bureau was also set up. Its purpose was to produce material which put across the government's view of the war. If necessary it could simply produce lies. One of the first pamphlets was Lord Bryce's *Report of Alleged German Atrocities*, which gave the impression that the German Army was systematically torturing Belgian civilians. It was published in 30 languages and told of such incidents as the public rape of 20 Belgian girls and of how eight German soldiers had bayoneted a young child. It was supposedly based on interviews taken from Belgian refugees in Britain but no evidence of these interviews has ever been found.

F Robert Graves, who served in the First World War until he was seriously injured by shrapnel in July 1916, commenting on the effects of the government's propaganda.

Propaganda reports of atrocities were, it was agreed, ridiculous. We no longer believed the highly-coloured accounts of German atrocities in Belgium.

G Lt-Colonel Rowland Feilding fought in the Battle of the Somme and actually watched the film while just a few miles behind the front line. He wrote an account of his experiences in 1929.

This battle film is really a wonderful and most realistic production, but must of necessity be wanting in that the battle is fought in silence, and moreover, that the most unpleasant part – the machine gun and rifle fire – is entirely eliminated. Of the actual 'frightfulness' of war all that one sees is the bursting of shells.

QUESTIONS

1 Study source A. Why was this report produced? Use sources A and D, and the text to explain your answer.

2 Study sources B and C. Why do you think these sources give different views of the activities of the German Army in Belgium? Use the sources and the text to explain your answer.

3 Source E a and b are both from the same film. Are they both equally reliable as evidence of the Battle of the Somme?

4 Are source E a and b equally useful to a historian studying British government propaganda?

5 'The British government was wrong to tell lies to its people during wartime.' Using the sources and your knowledge, explain whether you agree or disagree with this view.

Image and Reality

A Women of Britain Say Go. Official government posters took up the message begun by the White Feather Campaign, though in rather less aggressive tones.

The White Feather Campaign

Not all propaganda was the work of the government. In August 1914 Admiral Charles Fitzgerald founded the order of the White Feather. This encouraged women to go up to men who had not yet joined the army and to give them a white feather. This was a symbol of cowardice.

Advertising

Another form of unofficial propaganda was advertising. Since everyone was talking about the war, companies used the image of the war to sell their products. This advertising reinforced people's views of what the war was like.

B William Brooks, talking in 1993 about why he joined up in 1915.

Once war broke out the situation at home became awful, because people did not like to see men or lads of army age walking about in civilian clothing, or not in uniform of some sort, especially in a military town like Woolwich. Women were the worst. They would come up to you in the street and give you a white feather, or stick it in the lapel of your coat. A white feather is the sign of cowardice, so they meant you were a coward and that you should be in the army, doing your bit for king and country.

C Mitchell's Golden Dawn Cigarettes. This advertisement was produced in 1915.

D A section of British trench during the Battle of the Somme.

E **James Lovegrove recalled his brush with the White Feather Campaign when he was just 16.**

On my way to work one morning a group of women surrounded me. They started shouting and yelling at me, calling me all sorts of names for not being a soldier! Do you know what they did? They stuck a white feather in my coat, meaning I was a coward. Oh, I did feel dreadful, so ashamed.

I went to the recruiting office. The sergeant there couldn't stop laughing at me, saying things like "Looking for your father, sonny?", and "Come back next year when the war's over!" Well, I must have looked so crestfallen that he said "Let's check your measurements again". You see, I was five foot six inches and only about eight and a half stone. This time he made me out to be about six feet tall and twelve stone, at least, that is what he wrote down. All lies of course – but I was in!"

F **The Labour Party leader, Keir Hardie, issued this statement as soon as war broke out.**

The long-threatened European war is now upon us. You have never been consulted about this war. The workers of all countries must strain every nerve to prevent their Governments from committing them to war. Hold vast demonstrations against war, in London and in every industrial centre. There is no time to lose. Down with the rule of brute force! Down with war! Up with the peaceful rule of the people.

Conscientious objectors

Despite all the government's propaganda some men did not want to volunteer. These men were known as conscientious objectors or 'conshies'. Officially there were about 16 500 men who refused to fight in the war. Some were pacifists who through their religious beliefs felt that men should not kill one another. Most of these belonged to the Quaker group of Christians.

Other men, like Aneurin Bevan in Source H, were socialists. They believed it was wrong for British workers to kill German workers. They did not believe that Britain was 'their' country, but that the rich people owned it and that the war was only being fought because of a disagreement between the rich people of Britain and Germany. The Russian leader Lenin, who described a bayonet as a weapon with a worker at both ends, best summed up this view. Some conshies completely refused to serve in the war and were put in prison. Others agreed to serve in roles that did not involve fighting. Some became cooks or stretcher-bearers rescuing injured soldiers.

G Conscientious objectors working at Dartmoor Prison in Devon.

QUESTIONS

1 **Study sources C and D. What differences can you find between the image of a trench in source C and that in source D?**

2 **Why do you think these two sources give such different images of a trench?**

3 **Because it is inaccurate does this mean source C is of no use to the historian?**

4 **Study source F. Why does Keir Hardie oppose the war? Use the source and the text to explain your answer.**

5 **Study sources F and H. Do they agree about why the Labour Party opposed the war?**

6 **Do you think source F or source H are useful to a historian studying the reasons why conscientious objectors opposed the war?**

H **Jennie Lee, who became a Labour MP remembers the views of socialists during the war.**

Many Labour party members were pacifists, in the strict sense, but others, including my father, took the same stance as a nineteen-year-old South Wales miner, Aneurin Bevan, who, when brought before the local magistrates' court for failing to respond to his call-up papers said, "I am not and never have been a conscientious objector. I will fight, but I will choose my own enemy and my own battlefield and I won't have you do it for me."

8 | What was the Attitude of the British People Once the War was Over?

A Sybil Morrison remembers the reaction when the first Zeppelin was shot down on 3 September 1916.

It was like a big cigar I suppose and all of the bag part had caught fire . . . it was roaring with flames; blue, red, purple. And it seemed to come down slowly instead of falling down with a bang. And we knew that there were about 60 people in it . . . and that they were roasting to death. Of course you weren't supposed to feel any pity for your enemies, nevertheless I was appalled to see the kind, good-hearted British people dancing about in the streets at the sight of 60 people being burnt alive – clapping and singing and cheering. And my own friends – delighted. When I said I was appalled that anyone could be pleased to see such a terrible sight they said 'But they're Germans, they're the enemy' – not human beings.

In 1918, at the eleventh hour of the eleventh day of the eleventh month, an **armistice** came into effect. It had been signed six hours earlier. The war was over. Britain and the empire had lost almost 1 million men. Germany had lost 2 million. Not surprisingly it would be known as the Great War. How did people feel now that the war was over? Naturally some hated the Germans.

During the war shops which were owned by people with German names had been attacked. It was widely believed that German soldiers in Belgium were killing babies with their bayonets. The propaganda produced by the War Propaganda Bureau (page 39) had its effect on the British people. This hatred of Germans soon became a hatred of anyone thought to be foreign. In 1917 there were attacks on Jews in both Leeds and London.

C Vera Brittain, who had served as a nurse, writing in 1933.

When the sounds of victorious guns burst over London at 11 a.m. on November 11th 1918, the men and women who looked incredulously [unbelievingly] into each other's faces did not cry jubilantly: "We've won the War!" They only said "The War is over". Wherever we went a burst of enthusiastic cheering greeted our Red Cross uniform, and complete strangers adorned with wound stripes rushed up and shook me warmly by the hand.

B Richard Noschke was a German who had lived in Britain for 25 years and married an English woman. In 1915 he was sent to an internment camp in East London. He became the camp's gardener.

The railway line was running alongside the piece of garden with constant trains passing by, filled with soldiers who on every occasion used the most fearful language, drawing their bayonets and threatening us in the most frightful manner, and if they could have got out of their train, I am sure they would have murdered every one of us.

D Celebrations in London, November 1918. These celebrations continued for three days and in the end the police had to be sent in to break them up.

E Giving him rope. A British cartoon from *Punch*, 19 February 1919.

F An extract from the diary of Ernest Cooper, 11 November 1918.

Flags soon came out, and the bells began to ring and a few of us adjourned [went] to the Mayor's house and cracked some bottles of Fizz. An impromptu [unplanned] meeting was called and the Mayor read the official telegram from the Swan Balcony. Some soldiers came up on a wagon with the Kaiser in effigy [a model of the German Kaiser], which they tied to the Town Pump and burnt amidst cheers.

G The reaction of Rifleman Harold Clegg, who was in hospital in England on 11 November.

We were all sitting at our mid-day meal on November 11th, when the matron entered with a telegram in her hand ... It was a complete surprise to us to hear that the armistice had been signed. Somehow the news did not convey much to us; the fact that the war was ended was news that had come too late; it mattered little to most of those seated in the dining hall at Elswick whether the war finished or whether it continued for years ... Had the news come two years earlier it might have been of interest to us.

H Corporal Jessop, who fought in the Battle of the Somme.

More than anything I hated to see war-crippled men standing in the gutter selling matches. We had been promised a land fit for heroes; it took a hero to live in it. I'd never fight for my country again.

QUESTIONS

1 Study sources A and B. How do they give a different picture of attitudes to Germans during the war?

2 Study sources C and D. How do they give a different view of people's attitudes to the end of the war?

3 Study sources E and F. Why do you think they give a different view of people's attitudes to the end of the war?

4 Study source G. What does it suggest was the attitude of Britain to Germans once the war is over?

5 'The British people did not hate the Germans at the end of the war. They were simply glad the war was over.' How far do these sources go to support this interpretation?

A Eric Geddes, a government minister speaking in December 1918.

Germany is going to have to pay, and I personally have no doubt that we will get everything out of her that you can squeeze out of a lemon and a bit more. Not only all the gold, but all the silver and jewels should be handed over.

B Lloyd George, the Prime Minister, speaking to the House of Commons.

We want a peace which is just but not vindictive [full of revenge] ... Above all, we want to protect the future against a repetition of the horrors of this war.

C Treaty of Versailles.

D Harold Nicolson, who was one of the British delegates at the peace conference, writing in 1919.

We arrived determined that a Peace of justice and wisdom should be negotiated; we left the conference conscious that the treaties imposed upon our enemies were neither just nor wise.

Key Issue — **What was the attitude of the British people at the end of the war towards Germany and the Paris Peace Conference?**

While the fighting had stopped on 11 November 1918, it took much longer to produce a peace treaty. It was not until June 1919 that the Representatives of Germany were brought to the Hall of Mirrors at the Palace of Versailles, on the outskirts of Paris, to sign the treaty. There had been a great deal of discussion about how to punish Germany. The French wanted Germany to be heavily punished. Many people in England agreed with this view. They believed that Germany had started the war and so they should have to accept the consequences of their action.

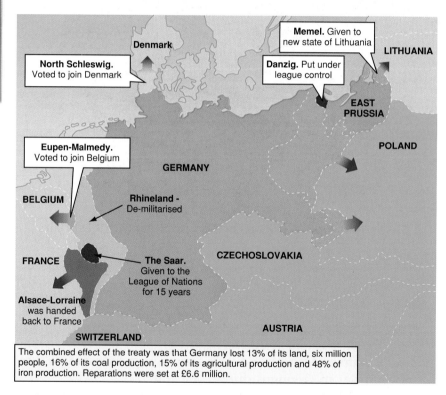

Memel. Given to new state of Lithuania

Danzig. Put under league control

North Schleswig. Voted to join Denmark

Eupen-Malmedy. Voted to join Belgium

Rhineland - De-militarised

The Saar. Given to the League of Nations for 15 years

Alsace-Lorraine was handed back to France

The combined effect of the treaty was that Germany lost 13% of its land, six million people, 16% of its coal production, 15% of its agricultural production and 48% of iron production. Reparations were set at £6.6 million.

The treaty included Article 231, the so-called War Guilt clause, which was used to justify the fact that Germany was going to have to pay for all the damage caused by both sides in France and Belgium. Although an exact figure was not set in the treaty, a figure of £6600 million was later decided. In public Lloyd George agreed that Germany needed to be punished. However in private he was worried about the effect this might have. Britain was a trading nation and Germany was one of its major trading partners. If Germany was bankrupted by the treaty British trade would suffer and Britain would become a less prosperous country.

Lloyd George was also worried by the spread of **communism**. In November 1917 the communists had taken control of Russia.

E A poster produced by the British Empire Union in January 1919.

F Two of the 20 million British wounded in the war.

Lloyd George was concerned that if the German people were reduced to poverty by the terms of the treaty, they too would turn to communism. Indeed a communist revolt had broken out in Berlin in January 1919, so these fears seemed very real. If Germany became communist, how long before Britain might follow?

The final treaty certainly did punish Germany, as source A shows. Germany also had its colonies taken away. These were to be ruled by Britain and the other victorious countries on behalf of the new League of Nations. Germany was also supposed to hand over its navy to the British. Rather than do this, the German navy sank its own ships while at the British naval base of Scapa Flow.

G John Maynard Keynes, writing in 1919. He was also a member of the British delegation at the conference. He resigned because he thought the terms were too harsh.

This chapter must be one of pessimism. The treaty includes no provisions for the economic rehabilitation [re-building] of Europe – nothing to make the defeated Central empires into good neighbours, nothing to stabilise the new states of Europe, nothing to reclaim Russia; nor does it promote in any way a compact [agreement] of economic solidarity amongst the Allies themselves.

QUESTIONS

1 Study source E. Why was this poster published in 1919?

2 Study source E. How reliable do you think it is about attitudes in Britain towards Germany? Use the source and your knowledge to explain your answer.

3 Study sources B and E. Why do they show a different attitude towards the treatment of Germany? Use the sources and the text to explain your answer.

4 According to source D, 'the Treaty of Versailles was neither just nor wise'. How do these sources show how this interpretation was reached? Use the sources and the text to explain your answer.

10 | How did British Society Change, 1906–1918?

A Lloyd George, commenting on the National Insurance Act in a speech in June 1911.

I never said the Bill was a final solution. I am not putting it forward as a complete remedy. It is one of a series. We are advancing on the road, but it is an essential part of the journey.

B Girls on motorbikes, 1925. Before the war girls would never have been seen dressed like this. It would also have been considered quite improper for them to smoke in public.

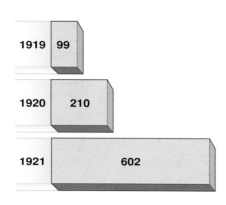

1919	99
1920	210
1921	602

C Numbers of women who qualified to be doctors in 1919, 1920 and 1921.

The Liberal reforms

By 1918 the standard of living of the very poorest had been improved. For example, old-age pensions meant that the aged could have a secure old age with a guaranteed income. Low-paid workers now got a minimum standard of medical care from the government but this didn't include their families. There was also unemployment benefit but only for 15 weeks.

The Children's Charter also made some progress towards improving the lives of poor children. They could get free school meals and scholarships allowed them to go to secondary schools without paying – but they had to pass an entrance examination first.

These reforms were only a first step but they showed the government was now prepared to take a leading role in improving people's standard of living.

Women – back in the cage?

Before the war a middle-class woman's place had been in the home. Women were considered to be a fragile species, in need of protection by and from men. Many working-class women had to go to work, but mainly in domestic service.

The war had given many women the opportunity to work for the first time. Perhaps more importantly it had given women the chance to work in jobs that previously had been reserved for men. However, once the war was over, men returned from the war and expected their jobs back. There was also no need for a massive munitions industry. By 1921 only 31 per cent of women had a paid job. In 1911 this figure had been 32 per cent.

But everything was not quite the same. The 1919 Sex Disqualification (Removal) Act allowed women to follow a career in medicine or the law. Furthermore, in 1918, women were at last allowed to vote, although they had to be aged 30 or more. It was not until 1928 that women were able to vote at 21, the same age as men.

Nevertheless, one major change was the social attitude to women. The war had seen single women able to go out on their own. They could smoke and drink in public. Skirts became shorter because women needed to be able to move easily at work. Young women in the 1920s did not return to pre-war behaviour. These young women were known as 'flappers'. They sometimes wore trousers and behaved like men.

The government

During the war the government had been forced to take great control of the lives of ordinary people. The government had run major sections of the economy, such as the railways and the mines, not to mention the powerful Ministry of Munitions. With the war over, the government abandoned most of these roles. The railways and mines were handed back to their owners. Most of the war ministries also ceased to exist. Those that survived no longer had their original function. During the war the Ministry of Labour had been able to direct the nation's workforce. After the war it was simply put in charge of unemployment.

In the short term things returned to pre-war ways. In the longer term the way the government was organised during the First World War provided a model for government in the Second World War. It would not take two years for conscription to be introduced the second time around.

In May 1915 the Liberal Prime Minister had abandoned single party government and formed a **coalition** with the other two main parties. This became the standard way for dealing with the crises which Britain faced in the first half of the twentieth century. A National Government was formed in 1931 to deal with the Depression. The Second World War also saw Britain governed by a coalition government.

Trade unions

During the war the trade union leaders had accepted dilution and the large numbers of women who took men's jobs. Many workers had been unhappy that the leaders no longer represented their interests, and so had elected shop stewards. These shop stewards were far more likely to call strikes than the official leaders, and they did not disappear once the war was over. The war had seen prices rise by 125 per cent. With peace, prices continued to rise. Workers now felt free to go on strike. They could no longer be accused of putting the country at risk. They wanted higher wages to cope with the rising prices.

The miners and the railway workers hoped for more than higher wages. They hoped that the government would now not just run these industries but own them as well. They felt that private owners did not look after the safety of the workers or pay enough money. They believed that the government would treat the workers much better.

D A slum in Nottingham. This was the sort of housing that the government was promising to replace. This photograph was taken in 1931.

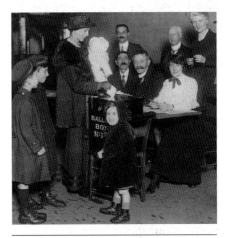

E Women vote for the first time in December 1918.

QUESTIONS

Using the sources and your own knowledge, explain how British society changed between 1906–18. You may want to organise your answer in the following sections.

a) The role of the government.

b) Social attitudes – did attitudes towards the role of women change?

c) Standard of living of the poor – how did it improve?

Glossary

armistice–a cease-fire between the armies at war

censored–the government checked all information before it was published. Nothing could be published if it was felt to be a danger to national security

census–every 10 years the government of Britain organises a survey of the people to see how society is changing

coalition–a government formed by two or more different parties

communism–the belief that socialism (see below) can only be achieved if the representatives of the workers seize control of the government.

conscription–the compulsory recruitment of men into the armed forces

dilution–semi-skilled and unskilled workers were allowed to do jobs which had previously only been carried out by skilled workers. Naturally skilled workers resented dilution

empire–a group of colonies under the rule of another country

friendly societies–for a small weekly payment friendly societies provided workers with money when they were ill

Industrial Revolution–the rapid development of British industry by use of machines in the early nineteenth century

propaganda–persuading people to believe in certain ideas and behave in a certain way; sometimes involves the telling of lies

socialist–a supporter of a system of government which supports greater government involvement in economy and society to help remove the differences between the rich and the poor

Trades Union Congress (TUC)–an official body which represents the trade unions in Britain

Index